MW01030905

Pancakes for Piggies

By Nina and Gianna Raqueño

Illustrated by Alexanda Carcich

Text copyright © 2011 by Nina & Gianna Raqueño

Illustrations copyright © 2011 by Alexandra Carcich

This first edition published by Petite Treats, Livonia, NY 14487.

ISBN-13:978-1479303212
ISBN-10:1479303216

Printed in the U.S.A.

The illustrations in this book were created using charcoal with water color washes. .

Book Design by Sharah Blankenship

# Pancakes for Piggies

By Nina & Gianna Raqueño

Illustrations by Alexandra Carcich

For my sticky, sweet, and itchy GG.

nce upon a time there lived 3 piggies. There was a big strong Daddy Piggy, a sweet Mommy Piggy, and a wee little GG Piggy.

One morning GG Piggy awoke and hurried downstairs to see what was for breakfast. With a wink Daddy asked, "What is my GG's tummy hungry for?" *He did not need to ask, for GG Piggy always asked for the same thing.*

"Maple syrup with pancakes, please," GG Piggy answered.

So Daddy started making pancakes and GG Piggy started to set the table.

Then all of a sudden GG Piggy started crying, "Weee weee weee!"

**M**ommy dropped her knitting and ran to GG and asked, "What's wrong dear GG?"

GG Piggy cried, "The maple syrup is almost GONE!"

*She was holding the jug upside down licking the last few drops.*

Mommy Piggy said, "Well now, we must just drop everything and go and collect some more maple sap right NOW!"

So Daddy Piggy left the pancakes on the table and off they went into the woods carrying their maple syrup buckets.

9

*N*ow, no sooner had they disappeared into the woods, when the big bad wolf appeared. With his nose to the wind he sniffed, "Yummmmmmmmmmm, pancakes and BACON, my favorite! It must be my lucky day since I just happen to have my first spring jug of maple syrup with me!" He sniffed and sniffed until his nose led him right to the piggies' door. "AHA! This must be the house of some tasty piggies."

*Knock Knock Knock.*

In his sweetest voice the wolf said, "Little piggies, little piggies, let me come in." But there was no answer. So he knocked again demanding, "Little piggies, little piggies, let me come IN!"

Nothing. Silence.

So he huffed, and then he huffed and puffed and the door flew right off the hinges and landed on the floor.

When the dust cleared, the wolf saw a table set with 3 stacks of pancakes, but NO piggies. Well, not wanting to **waste** the pancakes he decided to eat some while he waited for the BACON (ahem, piggies) to return.

Now, he was a great big wolf so he started with the biggest pile of pancakes. "**OUUCHH**!!," he cried as he burnt his tongue! He drank down some of his maple syrup to cool his tongue off. AHhhh! He tried the medium sized pile of pancakes. Brrrr! They were too cold and soggy. Then he tried the wee little pile of pancakes and before he noticed 1, 2, 3 they were all gone. Burp!

Then he decided to eat up those cold pancakes too 1, 2, 3, 4, 5. Burp! But he was still hungry so he poured his maple syrup all over the hot pancakes and gobbled them up too

1, 2, 3, 4, 5, 6, 7, 8, 9, BURP, 10!

As soon as he had eaten his 18th pancake, he started to moan and groan. "Why did I eat so many pancakes? Oh, I have a tummy ache... I need to sit and rest awhile and wait for the piggies to return."

So he ventured further into the home to see if he could find a comfy place to relax. He first tried the big chair, but it was too scratchy. "Who uses horsehair in their chairs anymore?" he muttered.

He then tried the medium chair for it looked all soft and comfy.

# YOUCH!

He came out of that chair quickly, as Mommy Piggy always left her knitting needles there.

$\mathcal{N}$ext he tried the wee little stool. It was so tiny he had to balance just so, or he would topple off. Finally, after practicing his balancing, he was able to rest for a while. Just when he thought his burnt tongue, bulging belly, and pierced bottom were feeling a bit better...

# CRACK!

Down went GG Piggy's stool into tiny bits and pieces.

"Oh what a rough day I have had," thought the wolf. "I think I need to lie down and rest while I wait for the BACON to come home."

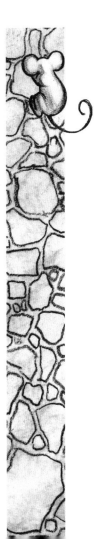

So he hobbled up the stairs. Now he was a great big wolf so naturally he tried the biggest bed first. He got all settled in and started to snore and then he started to wiggle and itch. He looked down at the scratchy bed made of straw.

Next, he wedged himself into the medium bed and fell fast asleep. He started dreaming and muttering "yum, bacon, a little smackerel, pancakes, smack, syrup…"

## AhChooo AhChooo AHCHOOO!

Poor wolf awoke sneezing out of control and he looked down at the bed. "Feathers! Why did it have to be goose feathers! The only thing I'm allergic to!"

He shook his head as he looked at the wee little bed. Then he rolled himself into a tight little ball, pried himself into GG Piggy's bed, and fell fast asleep. *Now he truly was the strangest thing you had ever seen, rolled up into a ball, covered with maple syrup, pancakes, horsehair, yarn, straw, and feathers!*

9

*L*ater the piggies returned with their maple sap buckets. Daddy Piggy said, "Did we forget to shut the door?"

But GG Piggy began to cry, "Wee wee wee! Our door has been broken!"

Mommy Piggy said, "Tsk Tsk, we can fix that. Now let's go figure out what happened here."

Mommy Piggy set the maple sap on the stove to boil down while Daddy and GG had a look around.

GG Piggy sobbed, "Our pancakes are ALL GONE!"

"Tsk Tsk," said Mommy Piggy, "we can always make more."

So they all started to search the house for clues.

Daddy Piggy grumbled, "Someone has been sitting in my chair!"

GG Piggy cried, "My chair is broken!"

Mommy Piggy exclaimed, "My KNITTING IS GONE!"

"Tsk Tsk," said GG Piggy, "you know you will knit MORE."

Now Daddy Piggy chuckled, but he agreed that something strange was really going on. So he crept up the sticky stairs.

Now just what did Daddy Piggy see? He was not sure. Was it a horse? A giant goose? A ball of yarnleftovers?? He rushed back down and whispered that he had found the strangest creature up in GG Piggy's bed.

Suddenly, GG had a marvelous idea, and she began to take charge. "Quick, Daddy, get the maple sap! Quick, Mommy, knit us up a net." They soaked the net in maple sap and then they all crept up the stairs.

Whoosh! They threw it onto the monster and it rolled out the window. It rolled and rolled and rolled right out of sight. They never knew what that odd creature was but at least they never saw it again. Phew!

The End.

"Wee wee wee," GG Piggy began to whine. "I'm still hungry."

So Daddy Piggy started to make some more pancakes, Mommy Piggy started fixing GG's chair, and GG Piggy set the table again.

GG Piggy was so hungry she ate 1, 2, 3, 4, 5, 6, 7, 8, 9, 10 pancakes.

Burp!

# Piggy Slippers

by Nina Raqueno [Ravelry ID: yarnleftovers]

## Supplies:

- Yarn: Pink worsted weight [Shown here in Manos Maxima color M2175 ]
- Approximate yardage: 100 yards
- Approximate Gauge: 20 sts per 4 inches [This is one time you don't need to fret over an exact gauge these slippers stretch and are very forgiving.]
- Knitting needles: size 6, 7, or 8
- Small amount of black yarn or embroidery floss for eye and nostril embellishment.
- Optional buttons for snout or eyes. [find Tagua Nut Buttons shown here: http://softexpressions.com]
- Tapestry needle for finishing

## Sizing:

Original pattern is written for a toddler which is shown in **BOLD**. Additional sizes shown in (child medium) (child large) (adult). The size may be adjusted by increasing or decreasing the

overall length of slipper and slightly adjusting the number of cast on stitches. Both the garter stitch and ribbing fabrics allow the slippers to stretch and can accommodate a range of sizes for ever growing feet.

## Some general foot length guidelines:

| | Age | Foot Length (inches) |
|---|---|---|
| Toddler | 2-4 | 5-6 |
| Child Medium | 5-8 | 6-7 |
| Child Large | 9-12 | 7-8 |
| Adult Woman | 13+ | 8-11 |

## Construction:

Slippers are knit flat, half in garter stitch and half in knit 1 purl 1 ribbing. Slipper is then folder in half and the back heel and top foot seams are sewn. Slippers may then be embellished with knitted ears, eyes, snout, and of course a curly piggy tail.

## Directions:

Cast On **28** (30) (34) (40) stitches. You may leave an approx. 18 inch tail for heel seam finishing.

## Back of Foot:

Row 1: Knit into the back of the first stitch, then Knit until 1 stitch remains bring yarn forward, and then slip the last stitch as if to purl.

(this process of knitting into the back of the first stitch and slipping the last stitch will create a nice top edge for the slipper opening.)

Repeat Row 1 for **28** (32) (36) (40) rows or **14** (16) (18) (20) garter stitch ridges.

## Front of Foot:

For the toe portion of foot you will switch to a knit one purl one rib.

All Rows: *K1, P1* across all stitches

Continue ribbing for **12** (15) (25) (30) rows.

## Toe Decrease:

R 1:  *Knit 1, Knit 2 tog* across entire row
R 2:  *Purl 1, Purl 2 tog* across entire row

Repeats rows 1 and 2 as necessary until you have approx. 8-10 stitches remaining.

### Momma Piggy Tip:

Not sure on what size to make for your little one? Have child stand on a piece of paper and closely trace the outline of their foot.

As you are knitting along you may periodically check the overall slipper length by simply laying it on top of this sketch. *Don't fret over the exact length. If the slippers initially appear to be too small try them on, you'll be surprised at how forgiving this pattern is. If they seem too large, don't fret for children's feet will undoubtedly grow.*

## Finishing:

Break yarn leaving an approximately 18 inch tail, run tail through all live toe stitches, and draw up tight. Fold slipper in half and use remaining tail to sew up top seam of slipper stopping seam where your garter ridge stitching begins.

Use cast-on tail or a yarn leftover to sew up back seam of slipper.

## Ears: (make 4)

Cast on 5 stitches leaving a ~12 inch tail that you will later use to attach the ear to the slipper.

R 1:   Knit across all stitches.

R 2:   Purl across all stitches.

R 3:   K1, increase 1 sts by knitting in the front and back of next stitch (kf&b), K1, kf&b, K1. [7 sts.]

R 4:   Purl across all stitches.

R 5:   K1, kf&b, K3, kf&b, K1. [9 sts.]

R 6:   Purl across all stitches.

R 7:   K3, slip 4th stitch, k2tog, psso, K3. [7 sts.]

R 8:   Purl across all stitches.

R 9:   K2, slip 3rd stitch, k2tog, psso, K2. [5 sts.]

R 10:  Purl across all stitches.

R 11:  K1, slip 2nd stitch, k2tog, psso, K1. [3 sts.]

R 12:  Slip 1st stitch, p2tog, psso. [1 st.]

Break yarn and weave in end. Use cast-on tail to attach bottom edge of ear onto slipper.

## Piggy Tails: (make 2)

Loosely Cast on 8 stitches leaving a ~12 inch tail. You will use this extra yarn to later attach the tail to the back of the piggy slipper.

R 1:   In each of the 8 stitches, knit in the front, knit in the back, and then KNIT IN THE FRONT AGAIN. [One stitch becomes 3 yielding 24 sts.]

R 2:   Bind off all stitches purlwise.

Break yarn and draw through the last stitch to finish and weave this end in. Use the cast on tail to attach spiral to back of piggy slipper.

## Momma Piggy Tip

When teaching a beginning knitter, Momma Piggy recommends using wood knitting needles and wool yarn. The stitches tend to not be so wild and slippery.

### Eyes & Snout:

Use some black yarnleftovers or embroidery floss to stitch eyes and nostrils. A spare button can also make a nice snout.

### Pass it on...

This is a super easy and forgiving project for a beginning knitter. Are you already an accomplished knitter? Consider teaching a youngster how to knit. This pattern starts right of with super easy garter stitch. By the time they have mastered the knit stitch it is time for the Knit 1 Purl 1 ribbing. You can reward them by constructing the ear and tail embellishments which require slightly more advanced techniques. What a fun project to work together on!

### Knitting Terms:

psso: pass slipped stitch over
k2tog: knit 2 stitches together
p2tog: purl 2 stitches together
slip: slip stitch purlwise
kf&b: an increase method of knitting into the front of a stitch and then also through the back of the stitch

Please find instructions for the kf&b stitch available online at: http://yarnleftovers.wordpress.com/techniques/

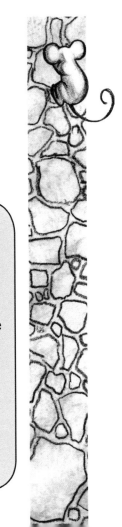

## About the Pattern:

Nina adapted her Mother's Christmas Mouse slipper pattern into these adorable piggies. She knew this slipper pattern must be truly quick and easy because for 40+ years her mom made a pair for each of her Kindergarten students! You always remember you Kindergarten Teacher and Jane's students certainly remember her and those gifted slippers. Long after the students graduated from Kindergarten they would stop her in the hallway to tell her their slippers still fit. That's the magical thing about the garter stitch and ribbing used in this pattern- they stretch and will grow as the child grows. So create some childhood memories and knit up a pair today.

15038739R00016

Made in the USA
Charleston, SC